RETURN OF THE BUNNY SUICIDES

GET IN LANE

EXISTENCE ⬇   OBLIVION ⬇

VALEAS MUNDUM

ANDY RILEY HAS WRITTEN FOR BLACK BOOKS, TRIGGER HAPPY TV, SO GRAHAM NORTON AND SMACK THE PONY. HE HAS CO-WRITTEN THE BAFTA AWARD-WINNING ROBBIE THE REINDEER, THE RADIO FOUR PANEL GAME THE 99p CHALLENGE AND THE FORTHCOMING DISNEY ANIMATION FEATURE, GNOMEO AND JULIET. HE DRAWS ROASTED, A WEEKLY COMIC STRIP IN THE OBSERVER MAGAZINE. ANDY IS THE AUTHOR OF THE BESTSELLING THE BOOK OF BUNNY SUICIDES.

RETURN OF THE BUNNY SUICIDES

ANDY RILEY

Hodder & Stoughton

COPYRIGHT © 2004 BY ANDY RILEY
FIRST PUBLISHED IN GREAT BRITAIN IN 2004 BY HODDER AND STOUGHTON
A DIVISION OF HODDER HEADLINE

THE RIGHT OF ANDY RILEY TO BE IDENTIFIED AS THE AUTHOR OF THE WORK HAS BEEN ASSERTED BY HIM IN ACCORDANCE WITH THE COPYRIGHT, DESIGNS AND PATENTS ACT 1988.

A HODDER AND STOUGHTON HARDBACK
10

A CIP CATALOGUE RECORD FOR THIS TITLE IS AVAILABLE FROM THE BRITISH LIBRARY
ISBN 0 340 83403 X

COVER AND PRELIMS DESIGN BY MARK ECOB
PRINTED AND BOUND IN SPAIN BY BOOK PRINT, S.L.
HODDER AND STOUGHTON
A DIVISION OF HODDER HEADLINE, 338 EUSTON ROAD, LONDON, NW1 3BH

WITH THANKS TO

KEVIN CECIL, ARTHUR MATHEWS, POLLY FABER, CAMILLA HORNBY, KATY FOLLAIN AND ALL AT HODDER & STOUGHTON, FREYA AYRES, DAVID AYRES.

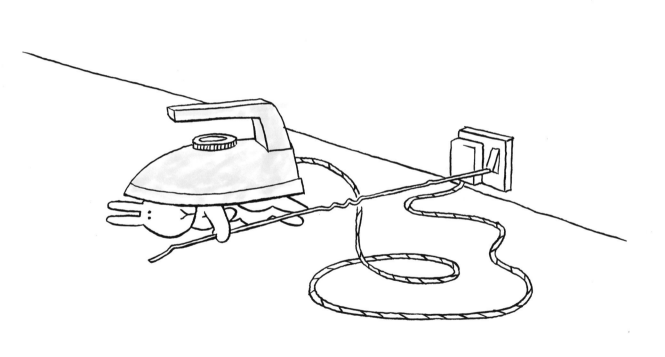

HARRY POTTER AND THE ORDER OF THE PHOENIX

HARDBACK

766 PAGES

ADD TO BASKET? GO

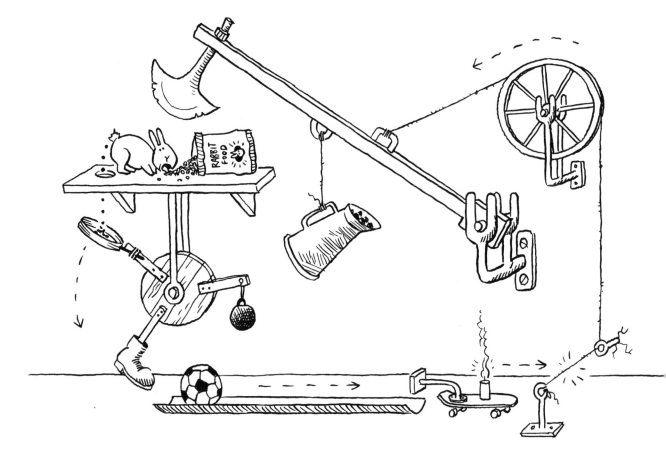

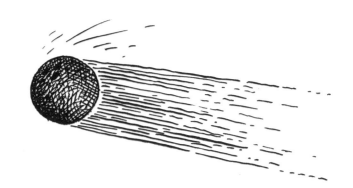

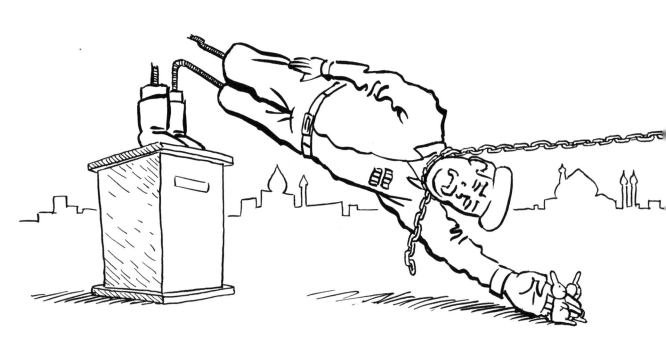

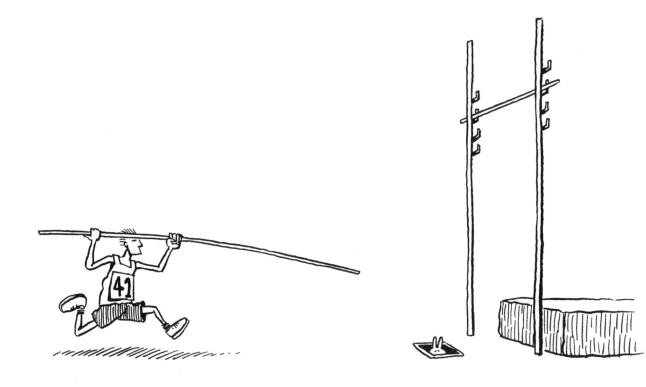

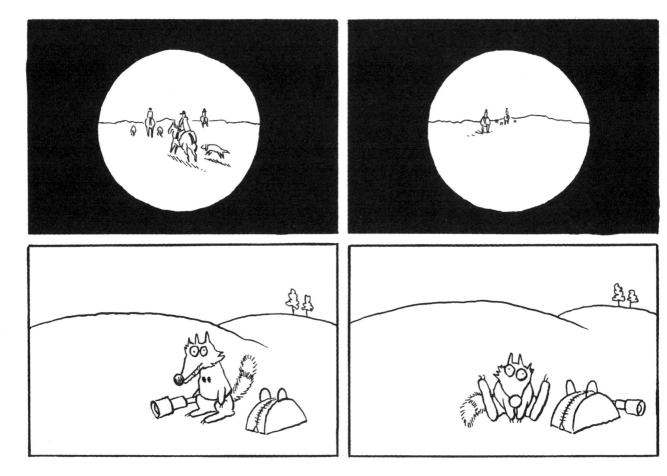

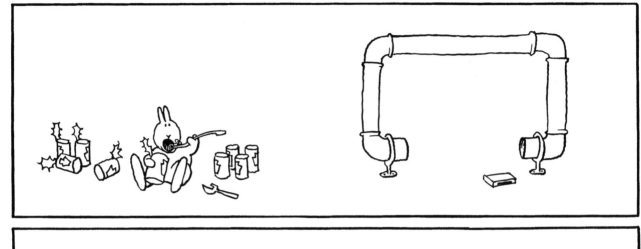
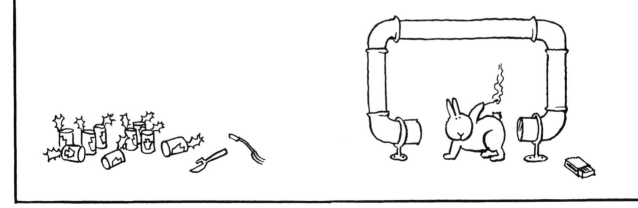

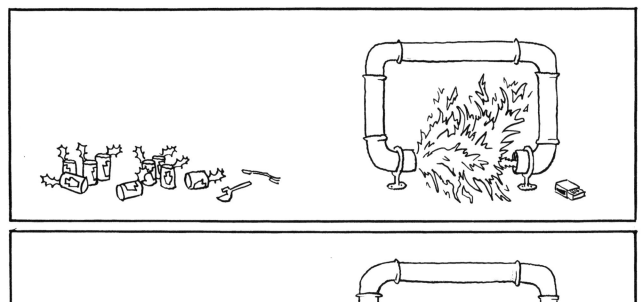
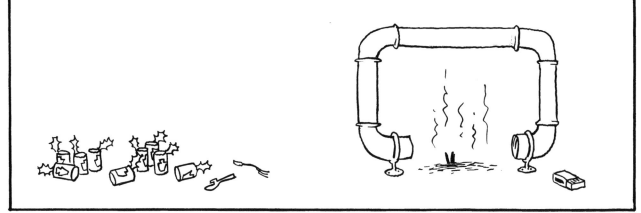

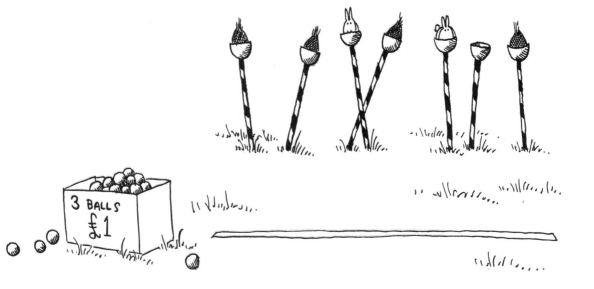

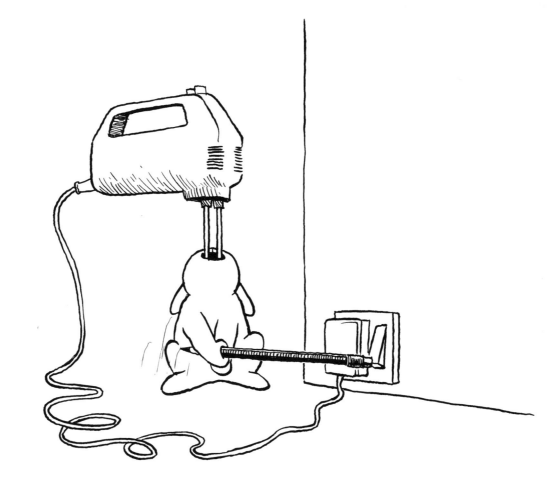

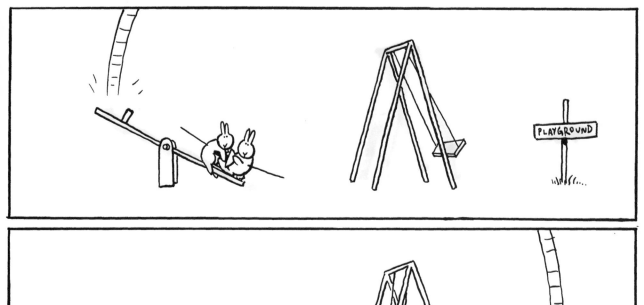